SUNSONG 1

Edited by
PAMELA MORDECAI
and
GRACE WALKER GORDON

Publishing for the Caribbean

For Cecil Gray

Addison Wesley Longman Limited
Edinburgh Gate, Harlow,
Essex CM20 2JE, England

Carlong Publishers (Caribbean) Limited
PO Box 489,
Kingston 10
33 Second Street
Newport West
Kingston 13
Jamaica

Lexicon Trinidad Limited
Boundary Road
San Juan
Trinidad

First published 1987
Seventeenth impression 1999

Set in 10/11 pt Ehrhardt Linotron 202

Printed in Singapore (JBW)

ISBN 0 582 76555 2

Contents

People and work

Tales that tell

Other worlds

Dear Teachers and Students

These poems come from all over the world and are of many different kinds: some are from the Bible, some are ballads (songs that tell a story), some are work songs, some are humorous, some are sad, some are dialect poems – we could go on and on. We took a long time choosing them because we wanted them to be of different kinds, telling about different experiences, making you feel different emotions – but most of all, we wanted you to *enjoy them and be able to understand them*. We hope we have managed to do that.

They are graded so that the ones at the end are a bit harder than the ones at the beginning. We've also written notes and questions on the poems to help you on the way. You will probably notice that we encourage you to read the lines and verses, and indeed the whole poem, again and again. We believe that because poetry is magical, that's the best way to enjoy it. A poem is sort of like a person. The first time you meet it, you can't expect to understand everything about it. The more you read it the better you'll know it and the more you'll probably like it.

We confess that here and there, there are some 'teaching' things. We've told you – as simply and easily as possible – about simile, metaphor, personification and alliteration. But they're not things to *know*; just hints on how a poem works, which you may find especially useful when you come to write your own poems.

We have suggested some things you might like to do with the poems in the classroom. These include dramatizing, miming, illustrating and writing. We hope you will find writing your own poems especially enjoyable.

If you have a tape recorder you will find it very useful. It is very important that the first time you hear a poem it should be read well. Try to find a good reader who understands the poem to do the first reading. If the reader is not a member of the class, this is where the tape recorder comes in handy. It is also very useful for listening to yourselves and improving your performances. You can keep your best recordings of poems on tape and share them with other classes.

We've given you some notes on each of the authors, too, so that you could see that they are ordinary people like you whose interest in poetry developed while they were young. Have fun – and if you wish, write to let us know what you think about the poems, or ask a question, or show us a poem of your own. Our address is c/o Longman Jamaica

Pam Mordecai and Grace Walker Gordon

Acknowledgements

We are grateful to the following copyright holders for permission to reproduce poems:

E. J. Arnold & Son Ltd for 'A Ballad of the Jericho Road' by F. Baker from *English Everywhere* Book 3. © 1979 Grame Kent; authors' agents for 'Jim' from *Cautionary Tales for Children* by Hillaire Belloc, pub. Gerald Duckworth & Co Ltd; Jonthan Cape Ltd for part poem 'The Little Boy and the Old Man' from *Light in the Attic* by Shel Silverstein; Doubleday & Co Inc for 'Happy New Year Anyway' by Joanna Cole from *A New Treasury of Children's Poetry* © 1984 by Joanna Cole; the Author, Grace Gordon-Walker for her poems 'Market Morning', 'The Pig's Tail', 'Rootsman: A Digging Song', 'The Sprat and the Jackfish'; William Heinemann Ltd for part poems 'What is Orange?', 'What is Black?' by Mary O'Neill from *Hailstones and Halibut Bones*; authors' agents on behalf of Lady Herbert for 'At the Theatre' by A. P. Herbert; Longman Group UK Ltd for 'Lament for Sam Sharpe' by Alma Norman from *Ballads of Jamaica*, 'Guilty Conscience' by Rodney Sivyour from *Let the Children Write* by Margaret Langdon; The New Yorker Magazine Inc. for 'Catalogue' by Rosalie Moore Brown from *The New Yorker* May 25, 1940. © 1940, 1968 The New Yorker Magazine Inc; Oxford University Press Inc. for part 2 of 'Folkways' by Edward Kamau Brathwaite from *Rights of Passage* (1967) © Oxford University Press 1967; the Author, Barnabus J. Ramon-Fortune for his poem 'The Riders'; Richard Rieu for 'The Flattered Flying Fish', 'The Old Wife and the Ghost' by E. V. Rieu. Copyright Richard Rieu; Sangsters Bookstores for 'New Scholar' by Louise Bennett from *Selected Poems* (1982); authors' agents for 'The Marrog by R. C. Scriven; the Author, May Swenson for her poem 'Southbound on the Freeway', Copyright © 1963 by May Swenson, having been originally published in *The New Yorker*; Susan Hamilton on behalf of the W. J. Turner Estate for 'Romance' by W. J. Turner; The University Society Inc. for 'Abou Ben Adhem' by Leigh Hunt from *The Bookshelf for Boys and Girls*, © N. C. Beasley; Viking Penguin Inc for 'Horse' from *Under the Tree* by Elizabeth Madox Roberts. Copyright 1922 by B. W. Huebsch Inc. Copyright renewed 1950 by Ivor S. Roberts. Copyright 1930 by The Viking Press Inc. Copyright renewed © 1958 by Ivor S. Roberts and The Viking Press Inc. and 'The Creation' by James Weldon Johnson from *God's Thrombones* Copyright 1927 by The Viking Press Inc. Copyright renewed 1955 by Grace Nail Johnson.

We have unfortunately been unable to trace the copyright holders of the following poems: 'Reflections on Wrecked Kites', 'Snakes and Ladders', 'Ballad of an Old Woman' by Frank Collymore; 'Week Fifty-One' by C.McG. Shake Keane; 'The Bazaars of Hyderbad' by Sarojini Naidu'; 'The David Jazz' by Edwin Mead Robinson, and would appreciate any information that would enable us to do so.

The Publishers are grateful to J. Allan Cash for their kind permission to reproduce the cover photograph.

Humour and story

New scholar
Louise Bennett

Good mahnin, Teacher – ow is yuh?
My name is Sarah Pool.
Dis is fi-me li bwoy Michael
An mi jus bring him a school.

5 Him bawn one rainy day, ma'am, it
Was comin awn to night –
Ugly baby grow pretty fi true,
For dis one was a sight.

Him bawn di week when Rufus
10 Jack-fruit tree did start fi bear,
Is dat same mont Oby pig dead
– But mi fegat di year.

We call him Mi, Mike, Mikey,
Jay, Jakey, Jacob, Jack,
15 But him right name is Michael Jacob
Alexander Black.

No treat him rough, yaw, Teacher,
Him is a sickly chile –
As you touch him hard him meck nize,
20 Some people seh him pwile.

Teck time wid him, yaw, Teacher –
If him rude an start fi rave
Dis beat another bwoy, an him
Wi frighten an behave.

25 For nuff time when him rude a-yard
An woan hear me noantall
Ah jus beat de bed-pose hard, mah,
An yuh waan fi hear Jack bawl.

Now dat yuh know him lickle ways
30 Ah not havin no fear Dat anyting wi mel him, so
Dat anyting wi mel him, so
Ah lef him in yuh care.

1 Why has Sarah Pool come to see the teacher?

2 What things in this poem make you laugh? Read the funny lines aloud.

3 Why are they funny? Did Sarah Pool intend them to be funny?

4 What can you tell from the poem about the kind of person Sarah Pool is? (Look at Verses 1, 2, 3 and 8).

5 How does she feel about her son? (Look at Verses 4, 5, 6 and 7).

6 Why do you think Michael Jacob Alexander Black has seven other names?

7 How do you think a) Mike   b) the teacher felt as they listened to Sarah Pool tell her story?

THE HON. LOUISE BENNETT-COVERLEY   is a distinguished Jamaican poet and performer who has composed and performed humorous verse in Jamaican Creole for many years. Her poems often use humour to point to follies and failings in the behaviour and points of view of ordinary and 'important' folk. Many of them are about current events and topical issues. Herself and Trinidadian Paul Keens-Douglas (see Book II) are the leading exponents of dialect poetry in the Caribbean.

The pig's tale
Grace Walker Gordon

Sir I was cooking my dinner
When *I* saw the neighbour's hog
Walk straight up to my cooking
And sniff it like a dog.

5   I warned that pig your honour,
Your honour I warned that pig.
I told him to leave my dinner
But the pig was acting big.

I told him 'Dog eat your supper
10 If you eat my food tonight,
If you touch my fish and ackee
I promise you, I will fight.'

I continued to cook my dinner
I ignored the stupid pig
15 But the hog was hard of hearing
And he didn't care a fig.

I was going to get the flour
And I'd hardly turned around
When I heard a big commotion
20 And my pot was on the ground.

You can't imagine, your honour
How it must really feel
To see a 'hard-ears' shoat pig
Treating your dinner like peel!

25 I'd not have been so angry
If it had been a dog,
But I couldn't stand the thought
of sharing dinner with a hog.

So I rushed out in great anger
30 And I gave a mighty shout
I threw my wooden spoon at him,
It caught him on the snout.

Would you believe your honour,
That the hog looked up and grunted,
35 Then he lay down and pretended
To be completely stunted?

So I thought he had a conscience
And in shame had hung his head.
But when I looked, your honour
40 The stupid pig was dead!

But as I said your honour
I warned the pig before.
I warned him once, I warned him twice.
I couldn't do much more!

45 A wise and clever judge therefore
Could not think it unfair
For me to clean and cook that pig
And eat him then and there.

And that's exactly what I did
50 It surely served him right
You can't ignore such warnings
And not expect a fight!

Just one more thing your honour
That pig was full of spite
55 For that pig made me suffer
From a belly-ache all night!

'Enough, enough, you've said enough
And silence in the court!'
His honour banged the table
60 To cut the laughter short.

'As I listened to you state your case
I understood your plight
But you have made one error
And so you can't be right.

65 That you had warned the creature
Is clear on every hand,
But why did you use a language
Which he did not understand?

5

To sum up, you took advantage
70　Of his inability
To comprehend a language
Which is plain to you and me.

The verdict then is 'Guilty' –
Yes, it is clear to me
75　That any wise or clever judge
Could not let you go free.

Pay a fine of twenty dollars
Or sixty days in jail
Give the man a pig or money,
80　Yes, sir, justice must prevail!

There's a moral to the story
Don't forget it any time
A pig is not a person
So don't cast your pearls to swine!

1　Where is the speaker in this poem? Who is he talking to? Why is
he telling his story? (verses 12, 15, 16, 19 especially).

2　Does anyone in the poem find the story amusing? Read the verse
which tells you the answer.

3　Do you find the story amusing? Why?

4　What do you suppose the storyteller wants the judge to do after
he has told him the story? (See verses 12, 13).

5　Read aloud the verse that tells you that the judge does not believe
the man's story.

6　Why did the judge say in verse 17 *don't cast your pearls to swine*?
(See St Matthew's Gospel Ch 7, verses 5 and 6. The reference to
the phrase from the Bible is termed an *allusion*. Try to find out
more about allusions.)

GRACE WALKER GORDON is a Jamaican teacher and author. She is a
former Lecturer in English at Mico Training College and taught
Language Arts in the (now defunct) In-Service Diploma in Education
programme at the University of the West Indies. She has worked
extensively in children's theatre and co-authored many Language Arts
textbooks for use at all levels in the educational system.

The David Jazz

Edwin Meade Robinson

David was a Young Blood, David was a striplin',
Looked like the Jungle Boy, yarned about by Kiplin' –
Looked like a Jungle Boy, sang like a bird,
Fought like a tiger when his temper got stirred.

5   David was a-tendin' the sheep for his Pa,
Somebody hollered to him – that was his Ma –
'Run down to camp with this little bitta snack,
Give it to your brothers, an' hurry right back.'

David took the luncheon, and off he hurried,
10 There he saw the Isra'lites lookin' right worried.
Asked 'em what's the matter – they pointed to the prairie –
There he saw a sight to make an elephant scary!
There he saw Goliath,
Champion o'Gath,

15 Howlin' in his anger,
Roarin' in his wrath;
Stronger than a lion,
Taller than a tree –
David had to tiptoe to reach to his knee!
20 'Come on,' says the giant, a-ragin' and a-stridin' –
'Drag out your champions from the holes where they're hidin',
Drag out your strong men from underneath their bunks,
And I'll give 'em to the buzzards, an' the lizards, an' the
    skunks.'

25 David heard him braggin', and he said, 'I declare,
The great big lummox got 'em buffaloed for fair.'
Goes to the brook, and he picks him out a pebble,
Smooth as a goose-egg an' hard as the debbil.
Starts for the giant, dancin' on his toes,
30 Whirlin' his sling-shot and singin' as he goes –
'Better get organised, for here I come a-hoppin',
Time's gettin' short, and hell am a-poppin'.
Hell am a-poppin' and trouble am a-brewin',
Nothin's going to save you from Big Red Ruin.
35 Trouble am a-brewin' and Death am distillin' –
Look out, you Philistine – there's gwine ter be a killin'!'

Giant looks at David an' he lets out a laugh –
Acts like a tiger bein' sassed by a calf;
Laughs like a hyena, grins from ear to ear,
40 Rattles on his armour with his ten-foot spear,
Starts out for David, bangin' and a-clankin' –
'Come on, l'il infant, you're a-goin' to get a spankin'!'
David takes his sling-shot, swings it round his head,
Lets fly a pebble – and the gi'nt drops dead!

45 *Moral*

Big men, little men, houses and cars,
Widders and winders and porcelain jars –
Nothin' ain't safe from damage an' shocks,
When the neighbourhood chillen gets to slingin' rocks!

1 Three verses in the poem tell you something about the kind of person David was. Read them aloud.

2 When something is compared to something else so as to better illustrate or show certain qualities about the first thing, the comparison is called a simile. Often you can spot a simile because the word 'like' or 'as' is used to make the comparison. Can you find any similes in the first verse? How do they help you to get a clearer picture of what David looked like?

3 Read the verse that tells you about David's size and Goliath's size.

4 What makes David decide to fight Goliath?

5 Why does the giant laugh? What happens after he laughs?

6 Why do you think the poem is called *The David Jazz*? (There are at least two reasons.)

7 Think of how a jazz band sounds. Now think of ways of using the different kinds of voices in your class to do a choral orchestration of this poem.

8

Jim

Who ran away from his nurse, and was eaten by a lion.

Hilaire Belloc

There was a boy whose name was Jim;
His friends were very good to him.
They gave him tea, and cakes, and jam,
And slices of delicious ham,
5 And chocolate with pink inside,
And little tricycles to ride,
And read him stories through and through,
And even took him to the zoo –
But there it was the dreadful fate
10 Befell him, which I now relate.

You know – at least you *ought* to know,
For I have often told you so –
That children never are allowed
To leave their nurses in a crowd;
15 Now this was Jim's especial foible,
He ran away when he was able,
And on this inauspicious day
He slipped his hand and ran away!
He hadn't gone a yard when –
                        Bang!

20 With open jaws, a lion sprang,
And hungrily began to eat
The boy: beginning at his feet.

Now, just imagine how it feels
When first your toes and then your heels
25 And then by gradual degrees,
Your shins and ankles, calves and knees,
Are slowly eaten, bit by bit.
No wonder Jim detested it!

No wonder that he shouted 'Hi!'
30 The honest keeper heard his cry,
Though very fat he almost ran
To help the little gentleman.
'Ponto!' he ordered as he came

35 (For Ponto was the lion's name),
'Ponto!' he cried, with angry frown.
'Let go, Sir! Down, Sir! Put it down!'

The lion made a sudden stop,
He let the dainty morsel drop,
40 And slunk reluctant to his cage,
Snarling with disappointed rage
But when he bent him over Jim,
The honest keeper's eyes were dim.
The lion having reached his head,
The miserable boy was dead!

45 When nurse informed his parents, they
Were more concerned than I can say: –
His Mother, as she dried her eyes,
Said, 'Well – it gives me no surprise,
He would not do as he was told!
50 His Father, who was self-controlled,
Bade all the children round attend
To James' miserable end,
And always keep ahold of Nurse
For fear of finding something worse.'

1 What was Jim's biggest fault? (verse 2)

2 What happened to him as a result of it?

3 Read the last three verses and say whether you think they were meant to make you laugh or cry. Give the reason for your answer.

4 What lines do you find particularly funny? Read them aloud.

5 Read verse 4 again. Now read the last two lines of the poem. What kind of person do they suggest Nurse was? Can you think of any worse experiences which Jim (or any little boy) might have encountered as a result of letting go of his nurse?

6 Try to say the poem in such an interesting way that those listening can re-live the experience.

HILAIRE (hill-air) BELLOC (1870–1953) was an English writer well known for his nonsensical verse and his books on history and travel. Born in France of a French mother and an English father, he attended English schools and Oxford University. He became a British subject in 1902 and served two terms as a Member of Parliament between 1906 and 1910. As a writer he is most renowned for his volumes of children's verse.

Ned Nott was shot

Ned Nott was shot
  and Sam Shott was not.
So it is better to be Shott
  than Nott.
5 Some say Nott
  was not shot.
But Shott says
  he shot Nott.
Either the shot Shott shot at Nott
10   was not shot,
    or
  Nott was shot.
If the shot Shott shot shot Nott,
  Nott was shot.
15 But if the shot Shott shot shot Shott,
  then Shott was shot,
  not Nott.
However,
  the shot Shott shot shot not Shott –
20   but Nott.

The fun in this tongue twister comes not only from the challenge to say it right but also from the play on the words 'not' and 'Nott', 'shot' and 'Shott'.

1 Who was shot? Who shot him?

2 Read the third and fourth lines of the poem. The sentence they make up has two meanings (one of which is ridiculous), when you hear it aloud. Write out the two meanings. Why is the ridiculous one ridiculous?

3 Read the poem with the appropriate emphasis on the words so that the audience can understand it. Read the last three lines, especially, very carefully. Say it as many times as you need to.

4 What do the rhythm and the sound of the words in the poem remind you of?

Limericks since Lear

A limerick is a comic poem with a particular shape. It is never more or less than five lines long. Limericks are funny because of tricks of pronunciation and peculiarities in spelling, and because of the situations or incidents which they describe. Puns also help to create humour in limericks. A 'pun' is a play on words in which two words sound alike but have different meanings. (They may have different spellings.) The fun comes from the confusion of the two possible meanings. The five limericks below are funny for different reasons. As is the case with many popular lyrics, the authors are not known.

A handsome young noble of Spain

A handsome young noble of Spain,
Met a lion one day in the rain.
   He ran in a fright
   With all of his might,
5 But the lion, he ran with his mane!

1 A handsome young noble of Spain

  a) Is this incident funny? Why?
  b) What does the expression '*with might and main*' mean?
  c) What is the lion's 'mane'?
  d) What is the play on words in the last line?
  e) Does the play on the words 'main' and 'mane' make the incident funnier?

A flea and a fly in a flue

A flea and a fly in a flue
Were imprisoned, so what could they do?
    Said the fly, 'Let us flee.'
    Said the flea, 'Let us fly.'
5   So they flew through a flaw in the flue.

2   A flea and a fly in a flue

   a) What is (a) *a flue* (b) *a flaw*?
   b) How many words in the poem can you find beginning with *fl*? This repetition of the same sound in a series of words is called *alliteration*. How does this use of alliteration help to make the limerick amusing?
   c) Can you find three pairs of words that have the same sound but different meanings? (One pair has the same spelling.)
   d) How is the play on words in this limerick different from the first one?

She frowned and called him Mr.

She frowned and called him Mr.
Because in sport he kr.
    And so, in spite,
    That very night
5   This Mr. kr. sr.

3   She frowned and called him Mr.
This limerick is a kind of puzzle.

   a) Of what word is Mr. the abbreviated form? Write out the whole word.
   b) If kr. and sr. rhyme with Mr. what do you think kr. and sr. stand for?
   c) Now read the limerick saying the words – not the abbreviations.

A epicure dining at Crewe

An epicure dining at Crewe
Once found a large mouse in his stew.
   Said the waiter, 'Don't shout
   And wave it about,
5   Or the rest will be wanting one, too!'

4   An epicure dining at Crewe

  a) Is it the play on words or the situation that makes this limerick funny?

  b) What would you normally expect a waiter to do about a mouse found in a customer's stew?

  c) Who is an epicure? Why do you think the writer used the word *epicure* rather than *customer*?

There was a young man of Bengal

There was a young man of Bengal
Who went to a fancy-dress ball.
   He went, just for fun,
   Dressed up as a bun,
5   And a dog ate him up in the hall.

5   There was a young man of Bengal

  a) Do you find this limerick funny? Why?

At the theatre

(To the lady behind me)

A.P. Herbert

Dear Madam, you have seen this play;
I never saw it till today.
You know the details of the plot,
But, let me tell you, I do not.
5 The author seeks to keep from me
The murderer's identity,
And you are not a friend of his
If you keep shouting who it is.
The actors in their funny way
10 Have several funny things to say,
But they do not amuse me more
If you have said them just before.
The merit of the drama lies,
I understand, in some surprise;
15 But the surprise must now be small
Since you have just foretold it all.
The lady you have brought with you
Is, I infer, a half-wit, too,
But I can understand the piece
20 Without assistance from your niece.
In short, foul woman, it would suit
Me just as well if you were mute;
In fact, to make my meaning plain,
I trust you will not speak again,
25 And – may I add one human touch? –
Don't breathe upon my neck so much.

1 Why is the speaker in the poem addressing the lady behind him/her?

2 Read aloud the four lines which sum up the way in which the lady behind the speaker has spoiled the play for the speaker.

3 What is a *half-wit*? How many *half-wits* does the speaker refer to? Who are they?

4 What does *mute* mean? Why would the speaker prefer the woman *mute*?

5 In what ways is the last line a human touch? Would you say it is the kindest line in the poem? Explain.

6 Which of the following words best describe
   a) the speaker,
   b) the lady behind him?
   rude   thoughtless   sarcastic   serious   foul

7 Can you read the poem to express the speaker's feelings?

ALAN PATRICK HERBERT was born in London, England in 1890. He studied to be a lawyer at Oxford University but never practiced law. In 1910 he began to write for Punch (magazine); in 1924 he became a member of the magazine's staff and worked there until he died in 1971. He was a copious writer, producing non-fiction, plays, novels and libretti for operas. He was also famous as a humorist and was often called 'the wittiest man of (his) time'.

Birds and Beasties

A tree toad loved a she-toad

A tree toad loved a she-toad
  That lived up in a tree.
She was a three-toed tree toad,
  But a two-toed toad was he.
5 The two-toed toad tried to win
  The she-toad's friendly nod,
For the two-toed toad loved the ground
  On which the three-toed toad trod.
But no matter how the two-toed tree toad tried,
10 He could not please her whim.
In her tree-toad bower,
  With her three-toed power,
The she-toad vetoed him.

This poem is a **tongue twister**. Its author is unknown. It is fun
because of the play on words and because of the challenge to say it
right. (e.g. You need to say *three* clearly or it will sound like *tree*.)

1 What do the following words mean?
  trod (1.8.) *whim* (1.10.) *bower* (1.11.) *vetoed* (1.12.)

2 Most of the lines rhyme at the end. Some, however, also have
  rhymes in the middle. (e.g. In 1.1, *tree toad* rhymes with *she-toad*.)
  Find all the lines that have a middle rhyme.

3 Why do you think the two-toed tree toad loved the three-toed
  she-toad?

4 In what way did the she-toad have power over the he-toad?

5 In what way did the she-toad *veto* the tree toad?

6 Is this poem about toads or does it tell you something about how
  people behave? Explain.

Soliloquy of a turkey
Paul Laurence Dunbar

There's a sort o' threatenin' feelin' in de blowin' o' de breeze,
    An' I's feelin' kind o' squeamish in de night;
I's a-walkin' round a-lookin' at de different style o' trees,
    An' a-measurin' dey thickness an' dey height.
5 For there's somethin' mighty 'spicious in de looks de darkies give,
    As dey pass me an' my family on de groun',
So it 'curs to me dat likely, if I cares to try an' live,
    It concerns me for to 'mence to look aroun'.

There's a curious kind o' shiver runnin' up an' down my back,
10   An' I feel my feathers rufflin' all de day,
An' my legs commence to tremble every blessed step I make;
    When I sees a axe, I turns my head away.
Folks is gorgin' me wid goodies, an' dey's treatin' me wid care,
    An' I's fat in spite of all dat I can do.
15 I's mistrustful o' de kindness dat's aroun' me everywhere,
    For it's just too good, an' frequent, to be true.

Snow's a-fallin' on de meadows, all aroun' me now is white,
    But I still keep on a-roostin' on de fence;
Isham comes an' feels my breastbone, an' he hefted me las'
20   night,
    An' he's gone aroun' a-grinnin' ever since.
'T ain't de snow dat makes me shiver; 't ain't de cold dat makes
    me shake;
'T ain't de winter-time itself dat's 'fectin' me;
25 But I think de time is comin', an' I'd better make a break,
    For to sit wid Mister Possum in his tree.

When you hear de darkies singin', an' de quarters all is gay,
    'T ain't de time for birds like me to be aroun';
When de hickory chips is flyin', an' de log's been carried away,
30   Den hit's dangerous to be roostin' nigh the groun'.

Grin on Isham! Sing on darkies! But I flap my wings an' go
    For de shelter of de very highest tree,
For dey's too much close attention . . . and dey's too much
    fallin' snow . . .
35 An' it's too nigh Christmas mornin' now for me.

(*darkies* American term for Black, usually working class people.
quarters places where workers live, as in 'slave quarters'.)   **19**

1 Why was the turkey examining the trees?

2 Why do the *darkies* or slaves seem suspicious to the turkey?

3 What special treatment is the turkey receiving and why is he mistrustful of it? Read the lines which support your answer.

4 Why has Isham gone around grinning since he felt the turkey's breastbone and hefted him?

5 What is causing the turkey to shiver and shake?

6 What time of year does verse 4 describe?
Why is it a dangerous time for the turkey?

7 What does the turkey finally decide to do?

8 Try reading the poem to express all that the turkey is feeling. Do his feelings change in the last verse? How?

PAUL LAURENCE DUNBAR (1872–1906) was the first nationally known black poet of America. He was extremely poor and when at age 21 he was employed as an assistant at the Haiti pavilion at the Chicago World's Fair, he spent every free moment trying to sell his first book of verse, *Oak and Ivy* to boost his $5 weekly wage. Dunbar wrote a great many poems, short stories and novels, but is best remembered for his dialect poems about the lives of poor black country folk. He died of tubercolosis.

Catalog
Rosalie Moore

Cats sleep fat and walk thin.
Cats, when they sleep, slump;
When they wake, pull in –
And where the plump's been
5   There's skin.
Cats walk thin.

Cats wait in a lump,
Jump in a streak.
Cats, when they jump, are sleek
10 As a grape slipping its skin –
They have technique.
Oh, cats don't creak.
They sneak.

Cats sleep fat.
15 They spread comfort beneath them
Like a good mat,
As if they picked the place
And then sat.

If male,
20 A cat is apt to sing upon a major scale:
This concert is for everybody, this
Is wholesale.
For a baton, he wields a tail.

(He is also found,
25 When happy, to resound
With an enclosed and private sound.)

A cat condenses.
He pulls in his tail to go under bridges,
And himself to go under fences.
30　Cats fit

In any size box or kit:
And if a large pumpkin grew under one,
He could arch over it.

When everyone else is just ready to go out,
35　The cat is just ready to come in.
He's not where he's been.
Cats sleep fat and walk thin.

1　Do you think this poet admires cats? Read the sections that
　illustrate your answer.

2　How would someone who dislikes cats describe the sound the
　male cat makes? How does this poem describe it?

3　Read the words, phrases, lines or verses that describe
　a) a moving cat　b) a cat at rest
　There are two similes in the poem, one describing how the cat
　moves, and the other, how the cat sleeps. Find and read them. Say
　whether you think they are effective.
　How does the repetition of the *s* sound (alliteration) help you to
　'see' the moving cat?

4　What is technique? What is the cat's technique?

5　Read the section that describes the cat's purr. Do you think it is
　a good description? Why?

6　What does *condense* mean? How does a cat condense?

7　What is a catalogue? Why do you think this poem is called *catalog*?

8　Try to read the poem to express admiration for cats.

9　Try to imagine a cat from the point of view of someone who hates
　cats. Now try to write some descriptive lines like the ones in this
　poem to express your hatred or disgust for cats.

ROSALIE MOORE (BROWN)　was born in Oakland, California in 1910
and educated at the University of California. She has worked in radio
and as a lecturer (in literary criticism), a piano teacher and a writer.
As Rosalie Brown she has written several books for children with her
husband, Bill Brown. She has received several awards for her poetry.

Horse
Elizabeth Roberts

His bridle hung around the post;
The sun and the leaves made spots come down;
I looked close at him through the fence;
The post was drab and he was brown.

5　His nose was long and hard and still,
And on his lip were specks like chalk,
But once he opened up his eyes,
And he began to talk.

He didn't talk out with his mouth;
10　He didn't talk with words or noise.
The talk was there along his nose;
It seemed and then it was.

He said the day was hot and slow,
He said he didn't like the flies;
15　They made him have to shake his skin,
And they got drowned in his eyes.

He said that drab was just about
The same as brown, but he was not
A post, he said, to hold a fence.
20　"I'm horse," he said, "that's what!"

And then he shut his eyes again.
As still as they had been before.
He said for me to run along
And not to bother him any more.

1 Read the words and phrases which tell you what the horse looked like to the speaker. How does the simile in line 6 help you see what the horse's lips looked like?

2 Why did the speaker have to look close at the horse through the fence?

3 Why did the horse have to explain that he was not a post to hold a fence?

4 Read the verses which tell you how the horse talked. What did he say?

5 If the horse didn't actually talk words how did the speaker hear what he said?

6 Which of the following do you think describes the reader's attitude towards the horse? Read the lines from the poem which support your answer.
a) admiration
b) respect
c) amazement
d) love
e) indifference

ELIZABETH MADOX ROBERTS was born in 1886 in Perryville, Kentucky and died in 1941 in Orlando, Florida. She was an educator, poet and novelist who grew up in the country parts of Kentucky. Her considerable reputation was built on novels in Kentucky settings: *The Time of Man, My Heart and My Flesh* and *The Great Meadow*. Many of her writings reveal her country background.

Donat

Pamela Mordecai

Donat is a bat: his feats are fantastic.
The first we will speak of
Are those called gymnastic;
For them he has earned some renown:
5   He can hang upside down
With his head to the ground
And his feet in the air!
He will stay there suspended like that –
He is truly a fine acrobat.

10   He is blind but his ears are astounding –
They will pick up the tiniest sounding;
And though he can't see,
He can hear where things are!
In fact you could say he has his own sonar
15   System built into his head.

There is one rather dread thing
About him – he bites
Both creatures and fruit
In the nights, which
20   Is really too bad
For his talent abounds
In things acrobatic
And hearing of sounds.

1 What do these words mean: feats (1.1), renown (1.4), suspended (1.8), astounding (1.10), sonar (1.14), abounds (1.21).

2 What two kinds of fantastic feats does Donat perform? Read the lines that describe these feats.

3 What is the one frightening thing about Donat?

4 What does the rhythm in the poem remind you of? Use your hands or arms or feet to tap the rhythm out.

PAMELA CLAIRE MORDECAI is a Jamaican poet who has written many poems for children. She is a former senior lecturer in English at Mico Training College and has worked extensively in radio and television. The author/co-author of many textbooks in Language Arts for use at all levels in the educational system, she now works in the Faculty of Education at the University of the West Indies, where she edits the *Caribbean Journal of Education*.

Nature

Extract from The Creation
James Weldon Johnson

Then the green grass sprouted,
And the little red flowers blossomed,
The pine tree pointed his finger to the sky,
And the oak spread out his arms,
The lakes cuddled down to the hollows of the ground,
And the rivers ran down to the seas;
And God smiled again,
And the rainbow appeared,
And curled itself around His shoulder.

Then God raised His arm and He waved His hand
Over the sea and over the land,
And He said, 'Bring forth! Bring forth!'
And quicker than God could drop His hand,
Fishes and fowls
And beasts and birds
Swam the rivers and the seas,
Roamed the forests and the woods,
And split the air with their wings.
And God said, 'That's good!'

1   As you read each line of this poem try to seen the action it describes taking place.

2   Which lines give you a sense of
    a) excitement
    b) satisfaction
    c) joy and well-being
    d) boundlessness

3   Read all the lines in which some aspect of nature is referred to as if it were a person. This is a poetic device called *personification*. Does this personification make the personified things clearer and more vivid? Give reasons for your answer.

4   Now do a choral orchestration of this poem using different voices to express each development.

JAMES WELDON JOHNSON   was a black American lawyer who was also a prolific poet, songwriter, novelist and university professor. Although he was not a believer, he is especially well-known in the Caribbean for his long poem *The Creation* which is an extraordinary recounting of the Biblical story of how God made the world. He died in an accident in 1938.

What is orange?
Mary O'Neill

Orange is a tiger lily,
A carrot,
A feather from
A parrot,
5 A flame,
The wildest colour
You can name.
Orange is a happy day
Saying good-bye
10 In a sunset that
Shocks the sky.
Orange is brave
Orange is bold
It's bittersweet
15 And marigold.
Orange is zip
Orange is dash
The brightest stripe
In a Roman sash.
20 Orange is an orange
Also a mango
Orange is music
Of the tango.
Orange is the fur
25 Of the fiery fox,
The brightest crayon
In the box.
And in the fall
When the leaves are turning
30 Orange is the smell
Of a bonfire burning . . .

1 According to the poem, what time of day is orange? Read the lines that give you the answer.

2 Read the lines that describe things that the poem says are orange.

3 What smell is orange, according to the poem?

4 What sound is orange, according to the poem?

5 What taste is orange, according to the poem?

6 What kind of behaviour can be described as orange, according to the poem?

7 Why do you think the poem says orange is *the wildest colour you can name*?

8 Try to make up a tune for the poem that would be orange or do an orange dance to the sound of the poem.

In questions 1 to 6 you identified various things which, according to the poem, are orange. In some cases these things are really coloured orange, like the mango and the orange. In some cases they are not – like the music and the happy day. In all cases, what the poet really means is that these things are *like* orange, except that, instead of saying orange is *like* a happy day, he says orange *is* a happy day. When a comparison is 'hidden' or not stated outright, in this way, we say it is a *metaphor*. Say in each case whether you think the poet is using a metaphor or not.

MARY O'NEILL was born in New York City and educated in Cleveland and at Michigan State University. She writes stories and articles as well as poetry and contributes to popular magazines like *McCalls, Good House-keeping* and *Women's Day.*

What is black?
Mary O'Neill

Black is the night
When there isn't a star
And you can't tell by looking
Where you are.
5   Black is a pail of paving tar.
Black is jet
And things you'd like to forget.
Black is a smokestack
Black is a cat,
10   A leopard, a raven,
A high silk hat.
The sound of black is
'Boom! Boom! Boom!'
Echoing in
15   An empty room.
Black is kind –
It covers up
The run-down street,
The broken cup.
20   Black is charcoal
And patio grill,
The soot spots on
The window sill.
Black is a feeling
25   Hard to explain
Like suffering but
Without the pain.

Black is licorice
And patent leather shoes
30   Black is the print
In the news.
Black is beauty
In its deepest form,
The darkest cloud
35   In a thunderstorm.
Think of what starlight
And lamplight would lack
Diamonds and fireflies
If they couldn't lean against
40   Black . . . . . .

32

1 Read all the lines in the poem that describe things you can see which are black.

2 Why is black kind? Read the lines that give you the answer.

3 What kind of feeling is black? Do you think it is a good feeling or a bad feeling?

4 What lines tell you about the sound of black? Talk about whether it is a good or bad sound.

5 Read the lines that describe a night that is black. Which of the following was this description meant to make you feel:
a) scared b) excited c) uneasy d) expectant

6 According to the poem, is black a beautiful colour? Read the lines that justify your answer.

7 Can you spot the metaphors in this poem? Talk about which things in the poem are *like* black rather than actually black, even though the poem says they are black. Remember these are metaphors. Say whether they are good metaphors.

Market morning
Grace Walker Gordon

Great gold pawpaws full and firm,
Fat swollen pumpkins come to full term,
Sleek green melons, bright pink when cut –
Unlike their cousin pumpkin who is gold in the gut.

5   Pearly green gungo peas dripping through my fingers,
Juicy golden mangoes with a pungent smell that lingers,
Pale yellow grapefruit and orange tangerines,
Crisp curled cabbages and green string beans.

Purple sweet potatoes piled upon the ground,
10   Grisly-looking yellow yams at sixty cents a pound,
Onion and escallion, garlic and thyme,
Sweet pepper, hot pepper, ginger and lime.

Irish potatoes earthbrown and heaped,
Scarlet tomatoes all freshly reaped,
15   Hanging hindquarters of beef bleeding red,
Goat-kid carcasses stiff-stone dead.

Green banana fingers and grinning cobs of corn
Call me to come on a cool clear morn,
To get for my meal of salad, soup or stew
20   Fresh meat, fruit and vegetables dripping with dew.

1 Read the lines that help you 'see' the goods in the market.

2 Read any lines which tell you how the person in the poem feels about going to the market.

3 What food items are spoken of as if they were persons? Explain how this use of personification helps you to 'see' these items more clearly.

4 Read aloud the verse you like best and say why you prefer it.

5 The repeated *k* sounds in the phrase *crisp curled cabbages* (1.8) is an example of alliteration – the same sound repeated in a series of words. Somehow the hard '*k*' sound helps to emphasize the crispness of the cabbages. Look through the poem for more examples of alliteration. Talk about what effect the repetition of each sound has on the reader.

Travel and far away places

Extract from # The child at play

R. L. Stevenson

I should like to rise and go
Where the golden apples grow;
Where below another sky
Parrot islands anchored lie,

5 Where in sunshine reaching out
Eastern cities, miles about
Are with mosque and minaret
Among sandy gardens set,
And rich goods from near and far

10 Hang for sale in the bazaar;
Where the Great Wall round China goes,
And on one side the desert blows,
And with bell and voice and drum,
Cities on the other hum;

15 Where the knotty crocodile
Lies and blinks in the Nile,
And the red flamingo flies
Hunting fish before his eyes;
Where in jungles, near and far,

20 Man-devouring tigers are,
Lying close and giving ear
Lest the hunt be drawing near
Or a comer-by be seen
Swinging in a palanquin.

1 What is a palanquin? In what country would you find one?
2 How many different places does the child wish to visit? Read the lines that support your answer.
3 What different sights does the child expect to see? Read the lines which tell you.
4 What do you think *parrot islands* are?
5 Why is the poem called *Child at Play*? Can you read it to express the mood or feeling of the child?

ROBERT LOUIS STEVENSON (1850–1894) was born in Scotland and wanted to be a writer from childhood. Although illness prevented him from attending school regularly, he entered university at the age of seventeen. He wrote constantly through his boyhood and youth in order to improve his style. Wherever he went he carried one book to read and one to write in. Although he was an invalid for more than 20 years of his life, he won fame as a writer of short stories, novels of adventure, essays and poetry.

Extract from Folkways
Edward Kamau Brathwaite

So come
quick cattle
train, lick
the long
5   rails: choo-
choo chatanoo-
ga, pick
the long
trail to town.

10   Come
come bugle
train
come quick
bugle
15   train, quick
quick bugle
train, black
boogie-
woogie wheels
20   fat
boogie-
woogie waggons
rat tat tat
on the flat-
25   out whispering rails
on the quick
click
boogie woogie
hooeee
30   boogie woogie
long long
boogie woogie
long long
hooey long
35   journey to town.

1   What does the rhythm of the poem remind you of? Where does it get faster? Where does it get slower? Why? Find and read aloud any examples of alliteration. What do the repeated sounds suggest?

2   What pictures do the lines *lick/the long/rails* and *pick/the long/trail to town* make you see?

3   Do you think the person in this poem is in a hurry to get to town or not? Read the lines which support your answer.

4   What does *boogie woogie* mean in each line in which it occurs?

5   What feelings do the last ten lines of the poem give you?

6   Do a choral orchestration to express the rhythm of the train and the feelings of the passenger.

EDWARD KAMAU BRATHWAITE was born in Barbados in 1930. His early education was in Barbados; afterwards he read History at Cambridge University in England. His first job as an educator in Ghana, West Africa, was a turning point in his life since it showed him vital connections between the language, culture and customs of West Africans and those of the peoples in the Caribbean. He is Professor of Social and Cultural History at the University of the West Indies and a distinguished literary critic as well as a poet and publisher. His publishing house is called Savacou Publications.

In the bazaars of Hyderabad
Sarojini Naidu

What do you sell, O ye merchants?
Richly your wares are displayed.
Turbans of crimson and silver,
Tunics of purple brocade,
5   Mirrors with panels of amber,
Daggers with handles of jade.

What do you weigh O ye vendors?
Saffron and lentil and rice.
What do you grind, O ye maidens?
10 Sandalwood, henna and spice.
What do you call, O ye pedlars?
Chessmen and ivory dice.

What do you make, O ye goldsmiths?
Wristlet and anklet and ring,
15 Bells for the feet of blue pigeons,
Frail as a dragon-fly's wing,
Girdles of gold for the dancers,
Scabbards of gold for the king.

What do you cry, O ye fruitmen?
20 Citron, pomegranate, and plum,
What do you play, O musicians?
Cither, sarangi, and drum.
What do you chant, O magicians?
Spells for aeons to come.

25 What do you weave, O ye flower-girls
With tassels of azure and red?
Crowns for the brow of a bridegroom,
Chaplets to garland his bed?
Sheets of white blossoms new-gathered
30 To perfume the sleep of the dead.

1   Find out the meanings of the following:
    a) bazaars   b) amber   c) jade   d) henna
    e) aeons   f) azure   g) chaplets   h) garland

2   In what country do you think the bazaars of Hyderabad are? Read
    the lines which mention items which help you to guess the answer.

3   Read aloud the lines which help you to see what each group of
    merchants is selling.

4   Which of the following qualities does the poem have? Support
    your answer with words or lines from the poem.
    a) magical   b) musical   c) strange   d) other-worldly

5   Do a choral orchestration to express the qualities of the poem as
    well as the feelings of the merchants and buyer. Arrange the
    voices in your class in groups ranging from low to high-pitched.
    Which lines of the poem would you assign to which group? Why?

6   What are the activities taking place in the bazaar? Read aloud the
    lines that describe them then try to imagine the different sellers
    and buyers engaged in each activity. You may want to illustrate
    the bazaar in a drawing or painting. Perhaps the whole class could
    create a collage or a wall-hanging to show the bazaar or a similar
    place like a market.

7   Try writing your own poem about a bazaar or market using a
    similar question and answer format.

SAROJINI NAIDU   lived from 1879 to 1949. Born in Hyderabad, she
was an Indian poet who took a leading part in social, educational and
political work on behalf of India. She became greatly involved in
welfare activities for women and children, travelled widely as a
lecturer and became the first Indian woman President of the Indian
National Congress. Her lyrical poetry, written in English, earned her
the title 'Nightingale of India'. Three volumes of her poems have
been published.

There was a naughty boy
John Keats

There was a naughty Boy
　A naughty Boy was he
He would not stop at home
He could not quiet be –
5　　He took
　　In his Knapsack
　　A Book
　　Full of vowels
　　And a shirt
10　　With some towels –
　　A slight cap
　　For night cap –
　　A hair brush
　　Comb ditto
15　　New Stockings
　　For old ones
　　Would split O!
　　This Knapsack
　　Tight at's back
20　　He rivetted close
And follow'd his Nose
　　To the North
　　To the North
And follow'd his nose
25　　To the North.

There was a naughty Boy
　And a naughty Boy was he
He ran away to Scotland
　The people for to see –
30　　There he found
　　That the ground
　　Was as hard
　　That a yard
　　Was as long,
35　　That a song
　　Was as merry,
　　That a cherry
　　Was as red –
　　That lead

40 Was as weighty
That forescore
Was as eighty
That a door
Was as wooden
45 As in England –
So he stood in
His shoes
And he wonder'd
He stood in his
50 Shoes and he wonder'd.

1 Read the lines from the poem which indicate the ways in which the boy was naughty.

2 Read the lines which tell you what he carried. What do you learn from them about the kind of boy he was?

3 Read the lines which tell why the boy ran away. What do those reasons for running away tell you about him?

4 What did he learn by running away?

5 Why do you think he stood in his shoes and wondered? Try to imagine and write down the thoughts of the boy as he stood in his shoes, wondering.

JOHN KEATS (1795–1821) was an English poet who became an orphan at age 14. At sixteen he was apprenticed to a surgeon and prepared to become a doctor. However he had a strong interest in literature and by age twenty-one devoted himself entirely to poetry. Keats eventually became one of the greatest poets of the Romantic era. He died of tubercolosis when he was only twenty-six.

Thinking about things

Happy New Year, anyway
Joanna Cole

January first isn't New Year's.
Everyone knows that.
The real new year is in September
when school starts.
5   January comes in the middle of the year,
when the edges of your notebook are all worn
and those new pencils with your name in gold
have been broken or borrowed or lost.
And your mother starts looking at your shoes
10 and saying, 'Are those getting too tight for you?'
Everything's old by January.
The teacher's long since stopped
playing games to learn your names
and asking how your summer was.
15 And you're right in the middle,
smack in the middle of the hardest math.
There's nothing new about January.
But your parents don't know that,
with their party horns and midnight kisses.
20 And they have the calendar on their side.
So Happy New Year, anyway.
You might as well pretend.

44

1 Who is the speaker in the poem?

2 Why does the speaker say that January 1st isn't New Year's? Read the lines that support your answer.

3 When does the new year start as far as the speaker is concerned?

4 To whom does 'everyone' in line 2 refer? Do you think line 2 contradicts line 18? Explain, reading lines from the poem to support your answer.

5 Who has the calendar on their side? Explain what this means.

6 What is the attitude of the speaker to saying 'Happy New Year'? Support your answer from the poem.

7 Talk about which of the following this poem is about. Read lines to support your answer.
   a) How times and seasons mean different things to different people
   b) A person who thinks about things rather than follows a custom blindly
   c) A person's reaction to a celebration which seems out of place
   d) How people do things without thinking about their effect on others.

JOANNA COLE   was born in New York, USA, in 1944. She graduated from the City University of New York, worked as an elementary school library teacher, and as a letters correspondent at Newsweek magazine. She became senior editor of books for young readers for the publishers, Doubleday and Co., and has written over twenty books of fiction and non-fiction for children.

Guilty conscience
Rodney Sivyour

I went to the shed for a cigarette.
Mind, I was not allowed to smoke, and if
dad caught me, there's no telling *what* would
happen.
5 I lit it.
And puffed.
What's that?
quick as a flash the cigarette is out and
I stand with beating heart, waiting.
10 It was only the door, swinging and
creaking in the evening breeze.
I lit up again.
And puffed.
The door opened with a push and a
15 clatter, hitting, storming, searching
out the sinner.
Without waiting to think I dashed out,
down the path, round the corner, and
indoors.
20 Safe?
Safe from myself?

1 Why did the person in the poem go the shed?

2 What would happen if his Dad caught him?

3 Why did he
   a) put the cigarette out,
   b) dash out of the shed?

4 Read the lines which tell you that the person had a guilty
   conscience.

5 In what respects did the door behave like a person? Do you think
   this is a good use of personification? Why?

6 Try to write a poem like this about a time when you did something
   wrong and were almost caught. Remember to use words that help
   the reader to 'see' and 'feel' your experience.

Snakes and ladders
Frank Collymore

Up and down the board they run,
Snakes and ladders. Snakes you shun,
Ladders there to climb upon.

So you throw the dice and play,
5   And when everything's O.K. –
Down you go the serpent's way.

Snakes and ladders, here, there,
Snakes and ladders everywhere,
And the reason isn't clear;

10 Only there they are. And so
Up and down... above... below,
Until you've made the final throw.

The illustration shows a picture of a snakes & ladders game.

1   Read the lines from the poem which tell you how the game is played.

2   What do the following stand for in the poem?
   a) the snakes
   b) the ladders
   c) the dice throws
   d) the final throw

3   Many poems use simple things to point to deeper truths about life. Do you think this poem does that? Explain.

4   a) Find the verse that tells you that catastrophes often happen when you least expect them.
   b) Find the verse that tells you that though life has good and bad things in it, people prefer the good things.
   c) Find the verse that says it's hard to understand why good things and bad things in life occur when they do.

5   Read the poem again. Talk about the poet's attitude to life. (Remember snakes and ladders is a game.) Which of the following do you think best decribes the poet's point of view
   a) pessimistic
   b) optimistic
   c) realistic
   d) ready for anything.

FRANK COLLYMORE   was a famous Barbadian poet, scholar, writer and editor. (We sometimes refer to such a person as a 'man of letters'.) He was born in Barbados in 1893, taught English at Combermere School for many years, and was editor of the important West Indian literary magazine, BIM, from 1943 until his death in 1963. He was honoured with an O.B.E. in 1958, and with an M.A. from the University of the West Indies in 1968.

Extract from Reflection on wrecked kites
Frank Collymore

On the sagging telephone wires
just outside my window
hang the corpses
of what were once
5 three joyous little kites.
Only a few days ago
they were describing
fussy little arcs
up there in the blue,
10 bobbing and buzzing
they soared as they flew.
And now
they look so forlorn,
so pitiful, hanging there limply,
15 their flat silly heads
woggling in the breeze,
their scraggy tails
twined around the swaying wires,
their happy function frustrated,
20 their brief day done.

1 Read the lines which help you to see the kites
   a) when they were new,
   b) now.

2 Think about the way kites move. What do lines 6–9 help you to
   see? What words help you to hear the sound of the kites in the
   air?

3 How is the function (purpose) of the kites frustrated?

4 The kites are personified, that is talked about as though they were
   persons, in several places in this poem. Can you find these
   examples of personification? Talk about whether they help to
   describe the plight of the little kites better.

5 To reflect is to think about things. What does this poem make you
   think about? What things could the kites stand for?

Extract from # Week fifty one
Ellsworth Mc G. Keane

Once the wind
said to the sea
I am sad
   And the sea said
5 Why
   And the wind said
Because I
am not blue like the sky
or like you
10 So the sea said What's
so sad about that
   Lots
of things are blue
or red or other colours too
15   but nothing
neither sea nor sky
can blow so strong
or sing so long as you
   And the sea looked sad
20 so the wind said
Why

1 Read the lines which tell you why the wind was sad.

2 Read the lines which tell you how the sea tried to help.

3 What happened to the sea in the end?

4 If you were the wind, what thing mentioned in the poem would you use to help cheer up the sea? Do you think it would work?

5 What is this poem really about? What do the sea and wind stand for?

6 What does the repetition of the *s* sound (alliteration) in the opening and closing lines of the poem help you to 'hear' and to imagine?

ELLSWORTH McGRANAHAN ('Shake') KEANE born in St. Vincent in 1927 is a musician as well as a poet. He was a high school teacher and also leader of an orchestra. He has worked with the BBC in England and in Germany he became co-founder with J. Harriot of Free Form Jazz. He is also a trumpeter and flugelhorn player. In 1975 he returned to St. Vincent and became Director of Culture there.

People and work

The Riders

Barnabas J. Ramón Fortuné

Over the hill in the mist of the morning
I see them a-coming, an army a-wheel;
Four abreast, six abreast, the road keeps on spawning
Them, hard-riding men with faces of steel.

5   Young men and old men, they ride on together,
None paying heed to the one at his side;
Toe to toe; wheel to wheel; crouched on the leather
Seats, over their handle-bars, onward they ride.

Grim must their faces be; theirs is the ride of life;
10   Bread's at the end of it, and leisure to follow;
Bread for a mother or sister or wife,
A toy for the kid, or a kiss in the Hollow.

Out of the distance and into the view they come,
Hundreds of men with their feet on the pedals;
15   The sweat on their faces; hear how their cycles hum,
Riding for bread, not for glory or medals.

(*The Hollow* is a depression in the Savanna in the city of Port of Spain which is
a favourite haunt of young lovers.)

1   What does the rhythm of this poem remind you of?

2   Line 2 in verse 1 describes the riders as an *army*. What two things
are being compared in this metaphor? Is it a good metaphor? Why?

3   Read aloud the third and fourth lines in verses one and two.
What do you have to do at the end of the third line in each of
the verses? What does this help you to feel?

4   Read all the lines which help you to see and hear the riders. Why
do you think the men are described as hard-riding men with faces
of steel? What else in the poem is steel?

5   Why are the men's faces grim? What is the reward for their ride?

6   Do a choral orchestration of this poem. What do you want to
express in it?

BARNABAS J. RAMÓN FORTUNÉ was born in Trinidad. He taught in
Primary School and at a Teachers' College before he migrated to
England in the early 1950's. He now teaches in England.

Ballad of an old woman
Frank Collymore

There was an old woman who never was wed;
Of twenty-one children was she brought to bed,
　　Singing Glory to God.

She gave them all her poor means could afford
5　And brought them all up in the fear of the Lord,
　　Singing Glory to God.

As soon as they grew up, each sailed away,
One after the other to the great U.S.A.,
　　Singing Glory to God.

10　Sometimes they thought of her, sometimes they wrote,
Sometimes they sent her a five dollar note:
　　Singing Glory to God.

And when in the course of the long waiting years
The letters ceased coming, she dried her tears,
15　　Singing Glory to God.

And when the old shed-roof collapsed from decay
She went to the almshouse and walked all the way,
　　Singing Glory to God.

And there she mothered many motherless brats
20　Who slept on her shoulder and pulled at her plaits,
　　Singing Glory to God.

Then one day she sickened and next day she died;
They brought out the hearse and put her inside
　　Singing Glory to God.

25　Only weeds and nettles spring up from her clay
Who is one with the Night and the Light of the Day.
　　Sing Glory to God.

A **ballad** is a poem that tells a story – often a sad story. Long ago ballads were songs and the verses followed a particular pattern. Many ballads had a refrain, which is a line repeated throughout the poem. Ballads were passed on from generation to generation by word of mouth. As they were passed on, people changed parts of the song so that there are often many versions of the same ballad. Many cowboy songs are ballads, and songs of this kind are still sung in many different parts of the world.

1   Which verses tell you something about the character of the old woman? Read them aloud.

2   What does the refrain *Singing Glory to God* tell you about the kind of person the old woman was?

3   Read the verses that tell you how the old woman's children treated her. Why do you think they behaved in this way?

4   Do you think this is a sad poem? Read the lines or verses from the poem that support your answer.

5   Use the different voices in the class to bring out the humour, drama and pathos (sadness) in the story, in a choral orchestration of the poem.

The little boy and the old man
Shel Silverstein

Said the little boy, 'Sometimes I drop my spoon.'
Said the little old man, 'I do that too.'
The little boy whispered, 'I wet my pants.'
'I do that too,' laughed the little old man.
5   Said the little boy, 'I often cry.'
The old man nodded, 'So do I.'
'But worst of all,' said the boy, 'it seems
Grown-ups don't pay attention to me.'
And he felt the warmth of a wrinkled old hand.
10   'I know what you mean,' said the little old man.

1   Read the lines which tell you all the ways in which the little boy
    and the old man were alike.

2   What concerned the little boy most?

3   What did the old man do when the little boy shared his worst
    problem? Why?

4   Is this poem in any way like the *Ballad of an Old Woman*? Read
    the lines which support your answer.

5   What do you think the people in the two poems needed most in
    life?

SHELL SILVERSTEIN was born in Chicago, Illinois, in 1932. He has
been a cartoonist, composer, lyricist, folksinger, writer – he has even
appeared in a movie. He has written and illustrated many books for
children and adults – indeed, his children's books often have a strong
appeal for adults as well. Many of his songs are available on record.
The Giving Tree, Where the Sidewalk Ends and *A Light In The Attic* are
among his highly successful books for children.

Lament for Sam Sharpe

Alma Norman

Chorus:
Toll the bell mournfully, mournfully, mournfully.
Toll the bell mournfully.
(Sam Sharpe is dead.)

Sam Sharpe listened and Sam Sharpe read.
5   Sam Sharpe heard what the planters said.
Sam Sharpe thrilled that 'Slavery dead.'

'Free paper soon,' thought Daddy Sharpe.
He told the others with singing heart
That days of freedom were soon to start.

10   But the months dragged on and no paper came.
'They're holding back freedom,' the men complain.
'Yu talk Daddy Sharpe, but yu talk in vain.'

Sam Sharpe listened and Sam Sharpe heard.
But Sam Sharpe doubted the planters' word.
15   And the seeds of liberty in him stirred.

'Down your tools,' he counselled then.
'And after Christmas be free, proud men.
Never work as slaves again.'

So two days after that Christmas day
20   The flames of freedom blazed out the way,
Burning down crops and mills, they say.

Up and down throughout St. James
On the mountain tops and plains
Slaves' defiance showed in flames.

25   But the planters' fearsome hand
Still lay heavy on the land.
Militia swooped with gun and brand.

From Trelawny and St. Ann
To St. James Militia ran.
30   Then the cruel revenge began.

56

Floggings fearsome to behold
Deaths too gruesome to be told
Fearful slaughter of the bold.

35 Daddy Sharpe was caught and tried.
'Rather dead, than slave!' he cried.
And for freedom's sake, he died.

Chorus:
Toll the bell mournfully, mournfully, mournfully.
Toll the bell mournfully.
(Sam Sharpe is dead.)

1 What was it that Daddy Sharpe *told the others with singing heart*? Explain *free paper*.

2 Why did the man say that Daddy Sharpe was talking *in vain*?

3 What stirred the *seeds of liberty* in Daddy Sharpe?

4 What did he counsel the other men to do?

5 Read the verses that describe what the slaves actually did. Read the verses that tell what the planters did in response to the slaves' action.

6 Explain line 20 and line 36.

7 Do a choral orchestration of this ballad to create moods of sadness, disappointment, excitement, terror, drama, where they seem appropriate. Talk about the best way to use the various voices in your class before you do the recitation.

ALMA NORMAN   is a Canadian who taught in Jamaica at Shortwood Teachers' College and at Calabar High School. She is married to a Jamaican and they now live in Canada.

Roots Man (for Jeremiah Davy)
(A Digging song)
Grace Walker Gordon

Some days I dig de groun. . . Uh-huh
Some days I plant de lan. . . Uh-huh
Some days I water de crops. . . Uh-huh
For I am a roots man. . . Uh-huh

5   And when de crops produce. . . Uh-huh
And when I reap de lan. . . Uh-huh
I know where de goods come from. . . Uh-huh
For I put in de roots man. . . Uh-huh

But when I think 'bout this man. . . Uh-huh
10   I don't know where I come from. . . Uh-huh
Some say I am African. . . Uh-huh
Some say I am Jamaican. . . Uh-huh

I want to know where I come from. . . Uh-huh
Does my life have a future plan?. . . Uh-huh
15   I want to know who plant this man. . . Uh-huh
I want to know my roots man!. . . Uh-huh

1 Read aloud the lines which tell you about the roots man's work.

2 What does he mean when he calls himself a *roots man* in verse 1?

3 In line 7, what are the goods referred to? How does the roots man know where they come from?

4 Who is *this man* in line 9?

5 What does the roots man want to know about himself? Explain the last line.

6 If you were the roots man performing this song do you think you might still be digging during the last two verses? Why? What would be appropriate body movement and tone of voice for a) the roots man b) the other workers, in the last two verses?

7 Think carefully about the roots man's questions and try to write a digging song which suggests the answers.

Tales that tell

The Flattered Flying-Fish
E.V. Rieu

Said the Shark to the Flying-Fish over the phone:
'Will you join me to-night? I am dining alone.
Let me order a nice little dinner for two!
And come as you are, in your shimmering blue.'

5   Said the Flying-Fish: 'Fancy remembering me,
And the dress that I wore at the Porpoises' tea!'
'How could I forget?' said the Shark in his guile:
'I expect you at eight!' and rang off with a smile.

She has powdered her nose; she has put on her things;
10   She is off with one flap of her luminous wings.
O little one, lovely, light-hearted and vain,
The Moon will not shine on your beauty again!

1 Why and how did the Shark flatter the Flying–Fish?

2 What one word in the poem describes the characteristic of the Flying-Fish which made it possible for her to be flattered?

3 Lines 3 and 4 of verse 2 are 'ironic' because they seen to mean one thing but really mean something else. What did the Shark want the Flying-Fish to think he meant? What did the Shark really mean? What did he intend to do? Find and read aloud other lines which are ironic.

4 What phrase in the poem tells you that the Shark deceived the Flying-Fish?

5 Which of the following do you think is the theme of this poem, that is, the main thing that the poem is about:
a) A shark and a flying fish
b) The danger of being vain
c) The danger of hearing only what is said and not what is intended.

6 How does the use of personification help you to discover that the poem is doing more than telling about the Shark and the Flying-Fish?

7 Read the second and third lines of the last verse a few times. What does the alliteration help you to see or hear? Do you think the alliteration in the title is effective? Why?

EMILE VICTOR RIEU (1887–1972) was a publishing executive, editor, translator and author. From 1912–1919 he lived in India working as manager of Oxford University Press there. He spent much of his life in publishing working at OUP, Methuen and Co. and eventually becoming editor of Penguin Classics. He was a member of the Joint Committee for the New Translation of the Bible and translated *The Four Gospels* as well as *The Odyssey* and Virgil's *Pastoral Poems*. He is well-known as a writer of poetry for children.

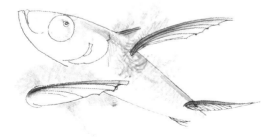

The Sprat and the Jackfish
Grace Walker Gordon

'Who cares if it's fair?'
the jackfish said,
flicking its fin,
flashing its head.

5   'It's nothing to me
that you found it first;
it's mine to keep
though you cry till you burst.'

The small sprat flapped
10 its silver tail
and thought, 'I wish
I were a whale.

I'd swallow this jackfish
with one gulp;
15 its body I would
turn to pulp.

Because you're just that much
bigger than me,
you think you're the ruler
20 of the sea!

Well, take my worm
it's yours all right –
in this unfair world
it's might that's right.'

25 'It's a juicy worm!'
the jackfish said,
flicking its fin,
flashing its head.

Then, choking and twisting,
30 tormented, it sped
along an invisible
line overhead ...

But the sprat did not see
as it went on its way
35 'It's an unfair world,'
was all it could say.

1 What were the Sprat and the Jackfish disputing over?

2 What was the Jackfish's attitude? Why did he have this attitude?

3 What was the only hope the Sprat had of solving the problem to its satisfaction?

4 Read the two lines which summarize one thing both the Sprat and the Jackfish believed.

5 In the end what happened to
a) the Jackfish
b) the Sprat?
Why did the Sprat say *It's an unfair world?*

6 There are several examples of alliteration in this poem. F, s and w are the sounds that are repeated. One of these examples occurs twice. Can you find them? Talk about whether the repetition of the sounds helps to make the story more vivid.

7 Does this poem do anything besides tell the story of the Sprat and the Jackfish? What do you think the following stand for?
a) the Sprat
b) the Jackfish
c) the invisible line.

8 In what ways are the poems Snakes and Ladders and The Sprat and The Jackfish similar?

The old wife and the ghost
E.V. Rieu

There was an old wife and she lived all alone
  In a cottage not far from Hitchin:
And one bright night, by the full moon light,
  Comes a ghost right into her kitchen.

5 About that kitchen neat and clean
    The ghost goes pottering round.
But the poor old wife is deaf as a boot
  And so hears never a sound.

The ghost blows up the kitchen fire,
10   As bold as bold can be;
He helps himself from the larder shelf,
  But never a sound hears she.

He blows on his hands to make them warm,
  And whistles aloud 'Whee-hee!'
15 But still as a sack the old soul lies
  And never a sound hears she.

From corner to corner he runs about,
  And into the cupboard he peeps;
He rattles the door and bumps on the floor,
20   But still the old wife sleeps.

Jangle and bang go the pots and pans,
  As he throws them all around;
And the plates and mugs and dishes and jugs,
  He flings them all to the ground.

25 Madly the ghost tears up and down
    And screams like a storm at sea;
And at last the old wife stirs in her bed –
  And it's 'Drat those mice,' says she.

Then the first cock crows and morning shows
30   And the troublesome ghost's away.
But oh! what a pickle the poor wife sees
  When she gets up next day.

'Them's tidy big mice,' the old wife thinks,
   And off she goes to Hitchin,
35   And a tidy big cat she fetches back
   To keep the mice from her kitchen.

1 What was wrong with the old wife?

2 What did the old wife find when she woke up?
   How did she try to remedy the trouble?

3 Do you think the simile in verse 4 is effective? Why? What does it
   help you to 'see'?

4 Can you find any examples of alliteration in this poem? Do they
   help you to 'see' or 'hear' more clearly, the things they describe?

5 Which of the following sayings do you think the poem illustrates?
   Read the verses or lines which support your answer:
   a) where ignorance is bliss it is folly to be wise.
   b) it's an ill wind that blows nobody any good.

6 What do you think is the best way to say this poem? Try it to see
   if it works.

7 Try to write a story about what happened on the night after the
   old lady bought the cat.

The blind men and the elephant
John Godfrey Saxe

It was six men of Hindustan,
To learning much inclined,
Who went to see the elephant,
(Though all of them were blind);
5   That each by observation
Might satisfy his mind.

The first approached the elephant,
And happening to fall
Against his broad and sturdy side,
10 At once began to bawl,
'Bless me, it seems the elephant
Is very like a wall.'

The second, feeling of his tusk,
Cried, 'Ho! what have we here
15 So very round and smooth and sharp?
To me 'tis mighty clear
This wonder of an elephant
Is very like a spear.'

The third approached the animal,
20 And happening to take
The squirming trunk within his hands,
Then boldly up and spake:
'I see,' quoth he, 'the elephant
Is very like a snake.'

25 The fourth stretched out his eager hand
And felt about the knee,
'What most this mighty beast is like
Is mighty plain,' quoth he;
'Tis clear enough the elephant
30 Is very like a tree.'

The fifth who chanced to touch the ear
Said, 'Even the blindest man
Can tell what this resembles most;
Deny the fact who can,
35 This marvel of an elephant
Is very like a fan.'

The sixth no sooner had begun
About the beast to grope
Than, seizing on the swinging tail
40 That fell within his scope,
'I see,' cried he, 'the elephant
Is very like a rope.'

And so these men of Hindustan
Disputed loud and long,
45 Each of his own opinion
Exceeding still and strong,
Though each was partly in the right,
And all were in the wrong!

1 What five characteristics can you learn from the poem about the six blind men of Hindustan? The poem says they were going to *see the elephant/(Though all of them were blind.)* Can you explain this?

2 Read aloud the verses which tell you what each observed about the elephant and the conclusion to which each came.

3 Read the simile which each blind man uses to describe what he thinks the elephant is like. Talk about whether each simile is a good comparison, that is, whether it helps to describe vividly, the particular part of the elephant which that blind man feels.

4 What happened as a result of their findings and why did this happen?

5 Is this poem merely about some blind men and an elephant? What do the blind men stand for? What does the elephant represent?

6 Read aloud any lines in the poem which suggest that a little learning is a dangerous thing.

JOHN GODFREY SAXE was born in Highgate, Vermont, USA in 1816. As well as being a journalist, poet and humorist, he was admitted to the New York bar, was a country superintendent of schools and was state's attorney of Vermont. He published many humorous poems and was much in demand as a humorous lecturer. After a series of personal tragedies, Saxe withdrew from society, sinking deeper and deeper into melancholy. He died in 1887.

A Ballad of the Jericho Road
F. Baker

An old man was walking in London one night
When along came some boys and they started a fight.
The old man was jostled and knocked on the head.
And one took his wallet and left him for dead.

5   Now as he lay there by the dustbins and cans
A policeman came by in a bullet-proof van.
He said, 'I'm off duty in ten minutes more –
Let the drunk sleep it off, it's no job for the law.'

The old man lay still in that alley so mean
10 When a rich man came by in a smart limousine.
He said, 'I must rush, I've a meeting at nine,
And that old man's woes are no business of mine.'

Then a man and his wife came along that dark street
And they stopped and they helped the old man to his feet.
15 'Come home and we'll bathe all your bruises,' they said.
'But we charge three pounds fifty for breakfast and bed.'

There's a moral to draw from this tale, I believe;
Try not to get set on by robbers and thieves.
Steer clear of dark alleys, I bid you take heed;
20 Samaritans now are a fast-dying breed.

---

1 What happened to the old man who was walking in London?

2 Read the lines which tell why a) the policeman, b) the rich man did not help him.

3 Read the lines which tell who helped him. Was this really help?

4 Who is a Samaritan? Why does the poet say *Samaritans are a fast dying breed*?

5 What is the biblical allusion in this passage (see Luke Chapter 10 verses 30–37). How is this story different from the one in the Bible?

6 Why do you think this poem is called *A ballad of the Jericho Road* rather than *A ballad of the good Samaritan*?

7 Try to say this ballad in a way which expresses the different ways in which the people responded to the old man. Talk about how the last verse should be read.

Other worlds

The Marrog
R.C. Scriven

My desk's at the back of the class
  And nobody, nobody knows
    I'm a Marrog from Mars
With a body of brass
5   And seventeen fingers and toes.

Wouldn't they shriek if they knew
  I've three eyes at the back of my head
    And my hair is bright purple
My nose is deep blue
10   And my teeth are half-yellow, half-red.

My five arms are silver, and spiked
  With knives on them sharper than spears.
I could go back right now if I liked –
  And return in a million light-years.

15 I could gobble them all
For I'm seven foot tall
  And I'm breathing green flames from my ears.

Wouldn't they yell if they knew,
  If they guessed that a Marrog was here?
20 Ha-ha, they haven't a clue –
    Or wouldn't they tremble with fear!
'Look, look; a Marrog'
  They'd all scream – and SMACK
The blackboard would fall and the ceiling would crack
25 And teacher would faint, I suppose.
But I grin to myself, sitting right at the back
  And nobody, nobody knows.

---

1 Read the lines that describe what the Marrog looks like. Do you
   find the description frightening? Give reasons for your answer.
2 Tap out the rhythm of the poem on your desk or on the floor.
   Which of the following best describes it   a) slow and scary
   b) fast and frolicsome   c) fast and frightening?
3 What colours are mentioned in the poem? Are they important in
   the description of the Marrog? Why?
4 Who, really, is the Marrog? How can you tell?
5 Read the poem in the way that you think the Marrog would have
   wanted it read. You may want to talk about this before you read it.
6 Try to draw a picture of the Marrog from Mars.

Southbound on the freeway
May Swenson

A tourist came in from Orbitville,
parked in the air, and said:

The creatures of this star
are made of metal and glass.

5   Through the transparent parts
you can see their guts.

Their feet are round and roll
on diagrams or long

measuring tapes, dark
10 with white lines.

They have four eyes.
The two in back are red.

Sometimes you can see a fine-eyed
one, with a red eye turning

15 on the top of his head.
He must be special –

The others respect him
and go slow

when he passes, winding
20 among them from behind.

They all hiss as they glide,
like inches, down the marked

tapes. Those soft shapes,
shadowy inside

25 The hard bodies – are they
their guts or their brains?

(A *freeway* is a busy motorway, with several lanes of traffic)

1 Where is the tourist in the poem from?

2 To what does *this star* refer?(1.3) From what point is the tourist looking at *this star*?

3 What creatures does he see? What are
   a) the transparent parts,
   b) the guts,
   c) their feet,
   d) their eyes,
   e) the diagrams or measuring tapes?

4 What is the *special, five-eyed* creature?

5 What are the soft shapes inside?

6 Close your eyes and imagine you are flying over your neighbourhood. Choose one familiar object and describe it as if you were the tourist from Orbitville.

MAY SWENSON was born in Logan, Utah, in 1919, and went to Utah State University. Her first book of poems, *Another Animal*, appeared in 1954. She writes for both adults and children and has won many awards for her poems, some of which have been set to music.

Excerpt from Job
(*Chapters 38 and 39*)

'Where were you when I laid the
  earth's foundation?
Tell me, if you understand.
Who marked off its dimensions? Surely
5 You know!
Who stretched a measuring line
  across it?
On what were its footings set,
  or who laid its cornerstone –
10 While the morning stars sang together
  and all the angels shouted for joy?

'Who shut up the sea behind doors
  when it burst forth from the womb,
when I made the clouds its garment
15 and wrapped it in thick darkness,
when I fixed limits for it
  and set its doors and bars in place,
when I said, 'This far you may come and no farther;
  here is where your proud waves halt'?

20 'Have you journeyed to the springs of the sea
  or walked in the recesses of the deep?

'Tell me, if you know all this.

'Does the rain have a father?
  Who fathers the drops of dew?

25 From whose womb comes the ice?
  Who gives birth to the frost from the heavens
when the waters become hard as stone,
  when the surface of the deep is frozen?

'Can you raise your voice to the clouds
30 and cover yourself with a flood of water?
Do you send the lightning bolts on their way?
  Do they report to you, 'Here we are'?
Who endowed the heart with wisdom
  or gave understanding to the mind?

35 Who has the wisdom to count the clouds?
    Who can tip over the water jars of
      the heavens
when the dust becomes hard
    and the clods of earth stick together?

40 'Do you hunt the prey for the lioness
    and satisfy the hunger of the lions
when they crouch in their dens
    or lie in wait in a thicket?
Who provides food for the raven
45 when its young cry out to God
    and wander about for lack of food?

'Do you know when the mountain
      goats give birth?
Do you watch when the doe bears
50   her fawn?
Do you count the months til they bear?
    Do you know the time they give birth?'

'Tell me if you know all this.'

1 Who do you think is speaking in the poem? How do you know?

2 Which line tells you that the creation of earth was an occasion for rejoicing?

3 What do you think are
a) the doors and bars that fix the limit of the sea
b) the springs of the sea
c) recesses of the deep?

4 Which lines describe the creator as a) mother b) father?

5 Read the lines that tell you the creator is concerned about living things. In what ways does he provide for them?

6 Read the lines that describe the breaking of a drought.

7 Why do you think this poem is a series of questions?

8 Do a choral orebestration of this selection from the Book of Job. Use the voices in your class to express the different qualities of the things described in the creation – e.g. the sea bursting forth, the thick darkness of clouds, the recesses of the deep, the water hard as stone etc.